Out of the Saddle

The Young Rider's Edition of Horse, Follow Closely

NATIVE AMERICAN HORSEMANSHIP™

BY GaWaNi Pony Boy

photographs by
Gabrielle Boiselle

BOWTIE
PRESS®

A DIVISION OF BOWTIE, INC.
www.bowtiepress.com

Ruth Berman, editor-in-chief
Nick Clemente, special consultant
Wendy Vinitsky, editor
Jacket and book design copyright © 1998 by Michele Lanci-Altomare

The people and horses in this book are referred to as *he*.

Library of Congress Cataloging-in-Publication Data

Library of Congress has already cataloged the hardcover edition as follows:
Pony Boy, GaWaNi, 1965-
    Out of the saddle : Native American horsemanship / GaWaNi Pony Boy ;photographs by Gabrielle Boiselle.
    p.   cm.
    Includes bibliographical references (p.   ).
    Summary: Describes how the Native American rider communicates with his horse while riding, on the ground, or out of the saddle.
Includes exercises for building a strong relationship with your horse.
    ISBN 1-889540-37-4 (alk. paper)
    1. Indians of North America-Domestic animals-Juvenile literature.   2. Horses-North America-Training-Juvenile literature.   3. Horsemanship-North America-Juvenile literature.
4. Human-animal relationships-North America-Juvenile literature.
[1. Indians of North America-Domestic animals.   2. Horses--Training.   3. Horsemanship.   4. Human-animal relationships.]
I. Boiselle, Gabrielle, ill.   II. Title.
E98.D67P68   1998
636.1'008997-dc21   97-36080
                                                     CIP
                                                     AC

Paperback ISBN: 1-889540-74-9

BowTie Press®
A Division of BowTie, Inc.
3 Burroughs
Irvine, California 92618

Manufactured in Singapore
First Printing November 1998
First Paperback Printing November 2002
Second Paperback Printing November 2005
10 9 8 7 6 5 4 3 2

Dedication

❖X❖X❖X❖X❖X❖X❖X❖X❖X❖

This book is dedicated to
Alexandra, Alivia, Lindsay, Neilly, Paige,
and made possible by Creator

—GaWaNi Pony Boy

Acknowledgments

❖X❖X❖X❖X❖X❖X❖X❖X❖X❖

A special thank you to
EquiSpeak Inc., Andrea Morrell,
Kathy, Mari, and Hawk

—GaWaNi Pony Boy

For more information on GaWaNi Pony Boy,
visit his Web site at
http://www.ponyboy.com

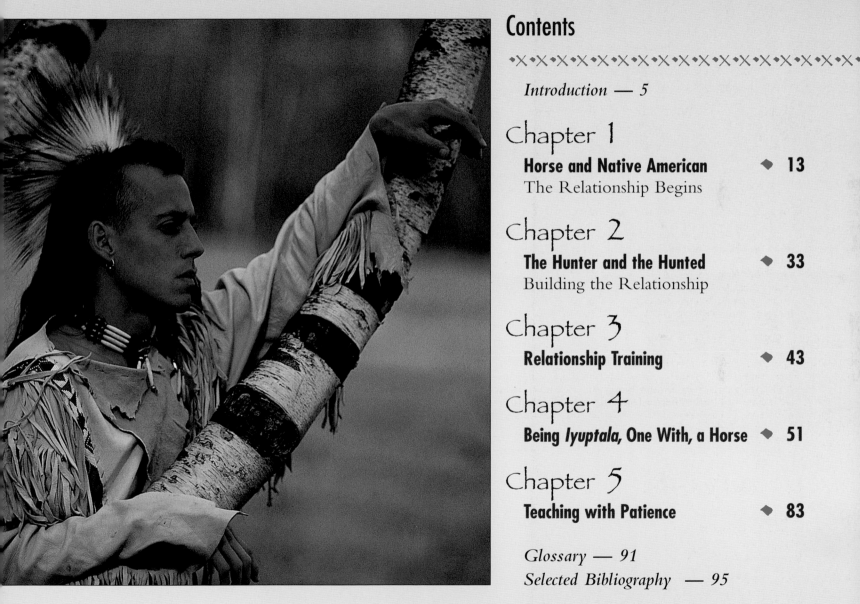

Contents

❖X❖X❖X❖X❖X❖X❖X❖X❖X❖X❖X❖X❖X❖X❖X❖X❖X❖X❖X❖

Native Americans were probably the greatest horsemen in American history.

Introduction

NATIVE AMERICANS WERE PROBABLY THE GREATEST HORSEMEN in American history. For 200 years, their skills and relationships with horses have been magic! They communicate with their horses while riding and while on the ground, or out of the saddle. This communication goes beyond what the average person accomplishes with a horse.

Do you want to know more about the special relationships Native Americans had with their horses? Then we must first look at the relationship that Native Americans had with all animals.

Silent Communication

One morning, I went outside to meet some friends. They were returning from a trail ride. One of them was riding a horse who had been taken from the wild. Their horse was a mustang. Suddenly, the mustang threw his head violently, breaking his bridle. I believe the horse saw this broken bridle as his chance to return to the wild. He bucked off his rider and raced down the road. I jumped on my horse Kola, who loves a good chase. But just as we were getting close to the mustang, the wild horse disappeared into someone's garage! At the same time, my reins got caught on a tree and were yanked out of my hands. Kola ran full speed into the garage, but this did not end the chase. There was another overhead door open on the other side of the garage. I picked up the reins and continued the chase.

Our adventure continued, and it included wooden fences, barbed wire fences, and split rail fences.

Listen!

Or your tongue will make you deaf.

—*Cherokee*

Luckily, we didn't have to jump the fences because the mustang had already bulldozed through them, clearing a path for us. After half a dozen near-death experiences for Kola and me, the mustang managed to find a pasture and stop. I was able to put a halter on him and call a vet to attend to his wounds.

I walked Kola back home over the same route we had first traveled. I saw all the obstacles we had negotiated together. We had been running on instinct with no time to consciously make the right maneuvers. Still, Kola understood my natural tendencies to lean toward and focus on the direction in which I wanted to go. I suddenly realized how much communication had taken place between Kola and me—and I didn't even have to say a word.

—GaWaNi Pony Boy

is my name
written in the Cherokee syllabary.
The syllabary was invented by
Sequoyah in the early 1800s.
**It is made up of 85 symbols that
represent units of sound
from spoken Cherokee.**
Although some of the symbols
look familiar to us,
the syllabary is different
from our alphabet.

I Am Related to Everyone

Sometime in the late 1500s, Europeans brought some new ideas to North America. Europeans told Native Americans that humans and nature are not related and that humans hold the highest position on earth. But according to Native Americans, all animals living on, in, or above Mother Earth are thought of as brothers and sisters. In other words, animals have been treated and respected by Native Americans in the same way Native Americans treat their brothers and sisters. This way of thinking has been expressed in the word *hunkapi* (hoon-KAH-pee), which means being related to everyone.

Most tribal members have viewed the brothers and sisters of the animal kingdom in one of three ways—as guides, as companions, and as creatures needing protection. Just as you look up to and seek advice from your older brother or sister, so have most Native tribes sought wisdom from animals viewed as guides. The friendship you have with your siblings is the same friendship Native Americans have had with companion animals such as dogs, cats, and horses. The responsibility you feel for a little brother or sister is the same sense of responsibility Native Americans have felt for those species, such as rabbits, needing to be protected. The Abenaki tribe has a story that gives us an idea of how Native Americans felt about animals.

According to Native Americans, all animals living on, in, or above Mother Earth are thought of as brothers and sisters.

Gluscabi and the Game Animals

(AN ABENAKI STORY)

Abenakis lived in eastern United States. Their name means "people of the dawn land."

Long ago, Gluscabi decided he would do some hunting. He took his bow and arrows and went into the woods. But all the animals saw him coming and hid from him.

Gluscabi could not find the animals. He was not pleased. He went home to the little lodge near the big water where he lived with Grandmother Woodchuck.

"Grandmother," he said, "make a game bag for me." So Grandmother Woodchuck took caribou hair and made him a game bag. She wove it together tight and strong, and it was a fine game bag. But when she gave it to Gluscabi, he threw it down.

"This is not good enough, Grandmother," he said. So she used moose hair and wove him another game bag, large and strong. She flattened porcupine quills with her teeth and she wove a design into the game bag to make it even more attractive.

But Gluscabi threw it down. "Grandmother," he said, "this is not good enough."

"Eh, Gluscabi," said Grandmother Woodchuck, "how can I please you? What kind of game bag do you want?"

Gluscabi smiled. "Ah, Grandmother," he said, "make one out of woodchuck hair."

So Grandmother Woodchuck pulled all of the hair from her belly. (To this day, woodchucks have no hair there.) She wove it into a magic game bag. No matter how much was put into it, there was still room for more.

Gluscabi smiled. "*Oleohneh*, Grandmother," he said. "I thank you." He went back into the woods and came to a large clearing. He called out as loudly as he could, "All you animals, listen to me. A terrible thing is going to happen. The sun is going to go out. The world is going to end, and everything is going to be destroyed."

The animals became frightened. They came to the clearing. "Gluscabi," they said, "what can we do? The world is going to be destroyed. How can we survive?"

Gluscabi smiled. "My friends," he said, "just climb into my game bag. You will be safe in there when the world is destroyed."

So all the animals went into his game bag. The rabbits and the squirrels went in, and the game bag stretched to hold them. The raccoons and the foxes went in, and the game bag stretched larger still. The deer and the caribou went in. The bears went in and the moose went in, and the game bag stretched to hold them all. Soon, all the animals in the world were in the bag. Gluscabi tied the top of the game bag, laughed, and slung it over his shoulder and went home.

"Grandmother," he said, "now we no longer have to look for food. Whenever we want anything to eat, we can just reach into my game bag."

Grandmother Woodchuck opened Gluscabi's game bag and looked inside. There were all the game animals in the world. "Oh, Gluscabi," she said, "you cannot keep all these animals in a bag. They will sicken and die. There will be none left for our children and our children's children. It is right that it should be difficult to hunt them. It makes you stronger by trying to find them, and the animals grow stronger and wiser trying to avoid being caught. This is the right balance."

"*Kaamoji*, Grandmother," said Gluscabi, "that is so." So he picked up his game bag and went back to the clearing. He opened it up. "All you animals," he called out, "you can come out now. Everything is all right. The world was destroyed, but I put it back together again."

All the animals came out of the magic game bag. They went back into the woods, and they are still there today because Gluscabi heard what his Grandmother Woodchuck had to say.

To Native Americans, horses were companions, messengers, teachers, and guides.

Chapter 1

Horse and Native American: The Relationship Begins

NATIVE AMERICANS RESPECT AND ADMIRE EVERY BIRD, FISH, rock, and plant just as you respect and admire close family members. If you have ever had a long-term relationship with an animal, you probably know the love that grows with this relationship. Horses have been viewed by Native Americans as companions and animals to be cared for. And sometimes the horse was also a messenger, teacher, or guide.

Native Americans lived for thousands of years without horses. Let's go back in time and find out how Native Americans first met the horse.

Ancestors of the horse lived in North America 40 million years ago. But 15,000 years ago during the Ice Age, the last of these prehistoric animals crossed a land bridge from what is now Alaska to Siberia. There, on the other side of the Pacific Ocean, they roamed over the grasslands of Asia and were domesticated.

Eventually, these domesticated horses were traded westward across Europe and North Africa. When the Spaniards came to explore the New World, they loaded horses onto boats and brought them to North America. Explorers Christopher Columbus, Ponce de León, and Hernando de Soto all brought horses with them.

A horse can travel more than 20 miles in a day.

Before horses were brought back to North America, Native Americans used dogs in everyday life. Dogs are loyal, good hunters, and they helped transport family belongings. Although Native Americans were never true nomads, some tribes moved from a summer camp to a winter camp. When moving, two large sticks were crossed and tied to a dog's back forming a travois on which family belongings could be tied.

Using dogs for moving wasn't easy. Can you imagine packing all your family's belongings and loading them onto a travois tied to your dog's back instead of getting a moving van? A dog can pack 30 to 40 pounds at best, and walk only 5 to 6 miles per day. And a dog needs to eat meat. Besides that, dogs often fight with each other, and if a rabbit should run across the path, a dog—along with all of his cargo—would take off after it.

The Native American Meets the Horse

When Native Americans first saw horses, they described them as being giant dogs. Throughout the Nations, the horse was called big dog, medicine dog, elk dog, spirit dog, and mysterious dog. Gradually, several Indian tribes began to understand the strange animals by watching how the Spaniards used them. But when Native Americans in New Mexico drove out the Spanish settlers and captured their sheep, cattle, and horses, they questioned the horse's value. After all, horses ate what little grass there was available for sheep. And it was the sheep, not horses, who could provide meat and wool. So the Southwestern tribes traded the horses to tribes in the north and east.

Many horses escaped captivity and migrated to an area that is now Idaho, Oregon, and Washington. Horses lived well in this region. Snow-capped mountains served as a natural fence line, guarding horses against such enemies as wolves and puma. All around were fields of green grass and mountain streams, so the horses had plenty to eat and drink.

Native peoples in these areas immediately saw how to use the horse to make life easier. A horse can carry 200 pounds on his back or drag 300 pounds on a travois. A horse can travel more than 20 miles a day and needs only grass to eat. And horses are relatively peaceful among themselves. Once tamed, horses were more dependable, easier to handle, and required less care than do dogs.

With the introduction of the horse, Native American life changed dramatically. On horseback, buffalo could be chased and hunted with great speed, increasing a hunter's chance of success. Hunting territories expanded with the increased ability to track, chase, and successfully hunt buffalo. Riderless horses were used as runners. Runners were trained to run, or chase, a herd of buffalo in the direction of the hunters while the hunters waited atop fresh mounts.

The Shoshoni tribe in Idaho was one of the first to see the value of having horses, but the Nez Percé quickly caught on. An unlikely people to even want horses because the Nez Percé mainly fished for salmon in the beautiful, clear north rivers, they simply liked the horse—especially the spotted ones. So some villages combined their resources and bought several from the Shoshoni.

The Nez Percé didn't waste any time. They began breeding their top mares with their top stallions. They wanted horses who were not only swift and surefooted but also calm and even-tempered. This was important in open country where there were no corrals or fences. This was also important for hunting and fighting in wars. A horse who is hard to control or flighty could cost his owner his life. For example, a horse who spooks at a deer is not one you'd want to take hunting. You wouldn't be able to get close enough to your prey to kill it.

Teaching and Training

✦×✦×✦×✦×✦×✦×✦×✦×✦×✦×✦×✦×✦×✦

Many people call me a horse trainer. I prefer to think of myself as more of a teacher than a trainer. The difference between teaching and training is that in teaching, the student learns something.

Your multiplication tables are a good example of teaching versus training. If you practice them over and over just to memorize them, you don't really learn why 2 x 2 = 4, but you know the answer. You have been trained to answer 4 when asked the question "What is 2 x 2?" If you really understand that 4 equals two sets of 2, then you have learned something. You have been taught.

Just as you can become bored memorizing multiplication tables, horses can become bored "memorizing" their exercises, going over them again and again. It is important to always try to teach rather than train an animal.

Good words
do not last long
unless they amount to something.

—*Nez Percé*

It's true that most horses can be trained, but the Nez Percé wanted their horses to have abilities of their own. Horses had to have a willingness to learn and be capable of developing loyal relationships. In one generation (about 20 years), the courageous Nez Percé became excellent horse people. It is written that the Nez Percé could ride bareback at full speed across rough countryside while firing bows and arrows.

The spotted horses who the Nez Percé liked so much came to be called Palousa, and finally they were named as we know them today—Appaloosa. The name is new; the breed is not. In fact, the breed can be traced back to 100 B.C. in China, where it was called the Heavenly Horse.

The Native American and His War Pony

Although most tribes did not corral or otherwise contain their horses, there was one exception: the war pony. Although a horse, it was called a pony by the French and English who were comparing the smaller war pony to their own huge draft horses who were bred to pull heavy wagons. Most Native warriors kept their ponies tied or hobbled close to the lodge at all times. Some warriors would even bring their ponies into the lodge during bad weather, forcing the women and children to sleep elsewhere. Sometimes when a warrior died, his war pony would be put to death alongside him as a sacrifice. Or sometimes when a horse was lost in war, the warrior would make a wooden sculpture of the horse and paint on the wounds that had killed him.

The war pony was chosen for his speed, agility, surefootedness, sensibility, endurance, and dependability. But above all, the pony was chosen for his temperament. The war pony had to have nerves of steel and the sense to "catch" a rider who has lost his balance. The pony needed unbridled speed and the ability to stand silently until led to do otherwise. More than anything, the war pony needed to be reliable. Mistakes in war meant lives lost.

Once they began to use and depend on horses, Native riders realized that their success and even their survival depended on the relationship they built with their horses. Native Americans knew that an understanding and strong relationship between human and horse is what builds reliability.

A warrior's ability to communicate with his horse was one of the most valuable skills he could develop. Children began to learn about horses at a young age. Two year olds were placed on a gentle horse and tied in the saddle. A six year old might get his own pony from his father or grandfather. By that age, he could already help herd the horses.

The Nez Percé wanted horses who were not only swift and surefooted but also calm and even-tempered.

Although Native riders worked 16 to 18 hours a day, they still found time to be with their horses.

Older boys competed in races and riding contests. They showed off their skill by hanging off the side of a galloping horse and scooping an object off the ground.

War ponies were trained by their riders, sometimes over many years. Looking back, we may think that in those days people had more time to work with their horses. Not true. They put in 16 to 18 hours of work each day to ensure their survival. Their work included hunting, cooking, cleaning, tanning hides, gathering nuts, berries, roots, and herbs. If you spend all day at school and play sports afterward, you probably have twice as much time left over for a horse than did the average Native American. But those horsemen understood that without a healthy working relationship with their horses, they had better not go to war.

The war pony was companion, best friend, soul mate, and teacher to the Native rider. Most important, the war pony was *kola*: a friend with whom you could face many enemies. The word *kola* is not normally used to describe animals but is reserved for human brother-warriors. In using *kola* to describe their relationship to their horses, Native American warriors are saying their horses are equals as brother-warriors.

The war pony was companion, best friend, soul mate, and teacher to the Native rider.

Native Americans painted special symbols on their horses.

Badge of Honor, Declaration of Courage

Native Americans painted their horses with special symbolic paints to intimidate the enemy, give their horses strength and courage in battle, and advertise the achievements of both rider and horse.

The medicine paint was made with natural ingredients: ash for white or gray; charcoal for black; berries for reds, blues, and purples; ocher for yellow. These ingredients were blended with either water or animal fat to make paint. The Plains warriors often painted the same symbols on themselves as they did on the flanks and necks of their horses. War paint was a badge or medal that indicated particular accomplishments, just like the badges you earn as a Girl or Boy Scout. Each symbol on the horse had its own meaning that was known to all members of the horse culture. A circle placed around the eye of the horse served to give the horse better vision. Upside down horseshoes indicated how many horse raids the rider had participated in. A design shaped like a keyhole placed on the horse by a medicine person or spiritual leader was a blessing and protector. Handprints indicated the number of enemies killed by the rider in hand-to-hand combat without the aid of weapons. Stacked horizontal lines counted *coup*.

Coup, a French word meaning touch, was a way of dishonoring the enemy by touching him. The belief that a warrior could obtain some of the soul of his enemy, as well as some of his strength, courage, and energy, motivated warriors to count coup whenever the opportunity arose. Coup did not always precede the death of the enemy but was sometimes used as a warning to the enemy to get out of tribal territory.

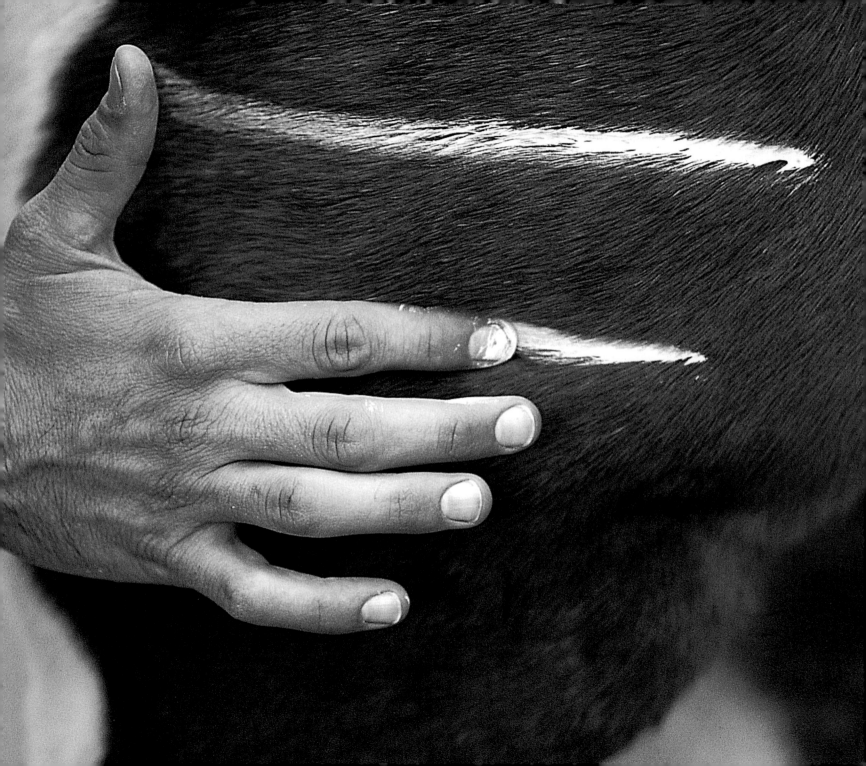

Feathers of war birds
or the riders own hair
would be woven into
a war pony's tail
and mane.

Native Americans also wove things into their war ponies' manes and tails. A lock of the rider's own hair was tied into the mane of his pony so their spirits could be one. A feather from a hawk, eagle, or falcon (all considered to be war birds) gave the horse the speed and agility of that bird. Hail marks, made famous by the Oglala Lakota warrior Crazy Horse, were believed to give the horse and rider the strength and fury of a great hail storm.

By being a partner with humans, the horse achieved a special status and was no longer a hunted animal. Horses who remained in the wild, however, needed to rely on their herd for protection and survival.

Hail marks were believed to give the horse and rider the strength and fury of a hail storm.

Animals can be put into one of two groups: they are either hunter or hunted. Humans are hunters— horses are hunted.

Chapter 2

The Hunter and the Hunted: Building the Relationship

ANIMALS CAN BE PUT INTO ONE OF TWO GROUPS: THEY ARE either hunter or hunted. This is one of the facts that determines their relationship with other species, including human beings. Horses are hunted—humans are hunters. Humans look like hunters, act like hunters, move like hunters, sound like hunters, and even smell like hunters. From a horse's point of view, you could have him for dinner at any given moment. To develop a close relationship, the hunter must earn a certain amount of respect from the hunted.

Horses also are herd animals. They spend most of their lives defending their position within the herd. Each herd member constantly

33

challenges the leadership abilities of other higher ranking herd members. Behavior of a herd animal, especially an animal who is the boss of the herd, can seem like predator behavior. Biting, kicking, chasing, and stomping occur often in a herd as the ever changing pecking order is challenged. This constant challenging of rank ensures that the strongest horses are given the highest positions in the herd.

Have you ever noticed how animals such as birds, fish, and horses who live in groups know how to move or change direction at the same time? It's a matter of focus. Members of a flock of birds, school of fish, or herd of horses are aware of what their leaders are focusing on. Many individual horses acting as one large herd is frightening and confusing to predators. By becoming one with the others in the herd, each individual enjoys the safety that comes from being a part of a larger whole.

Follow the Itancan

Native American riders knew that most of the horse's nature stems from the horse being a herd animal. In a herd, the *itancan* (ee-TAHN-chun), or leader, leads, and all other members of the herd, *waunca* (wah-OON-kah), follow. The herd knows the itancan has their best interests in mind. If you have a horse, you can become the itancan of your two-member herd.

Once you become the itancan, it will be natural for your horse to follow your lead. Your horse will know you have his best interests in mind.

It is important you understand how waunca thinks. Waunca must follow itancan without questioning itancan's actions. If waunca did not blindly follow itancan, the purpose of the herd would be defeated and eventually the species would die out. You have already heard the saying "you can lead a horse to water but you can't make him drink." With the relationship between itancan and waunca, it is possible to lead a horse to drink. Here's how.

When a herd of horses approaches a watering hole, the itancan is always the first horse to reach the water. The itancan checks for danger then takes a few sips. Only then will the rest of the herd drink its fill, as the itancan backs off and watches for predators. After the herd has finished drinking and the itancan feels all is safe, then—and only then— will he go back to the water and drink until his thirst is quenched. The itancan has led horses to water and led them to drink.

Once you are the itancan of your herd, your horse will always look to you for guidance and direction. You must not only give the animal a reason to feel secure, but you must always maintain the status of leader, or itancan, in the herd—a herd of two, rider and horse. This can be tricky.

For example, have you ever felt that your dog is getting spoiled? Perhaps she's become too used to getting treats from the table and is ignoring her regular food, or maybe you've let her up on the living room couch too often and now she climbs up without even asking! If a pet is acting spoiled, you are probably losing your status as itancan of your two-member herd, or in this case, pack. Your pet is doing nothing more than getting comfortable with, and enjoying, her new status. In the very beginning of developing the relationship, it is important for you to be the leader your pet is looking for.

Many people look at animals as being furry people. Native Americans understood that a horse is a horse, which helps explain why Native American riders were so successful with horses. Looking at the horse, Native Americans defined its nature and treated horses according

Native Americans were successful with horses because they understood that a horse is a horse, not a furry person.

To develop strong relationships with animals, we must understand that all life is connected.

to that definition. They did not attempt to treat the horse as they would a dog or a human, but instead they trained, rode, and communicated within the boundaries set forth by the nature of the horse.

To develop strong relationships with other animals, we must understand that all life is connected. We, as humans, must treat the animals of our larger family with respect. The winged animals of the air, the four-leggeds on the land, and the fish in the waters are our brothers and sisters. Once we realize this and act out our understanding of this relationship, and once we accept the responsibility to all our animal brothers and sisters, then true learning can begin. Here is a story from the Cherokee that describes how all life is connected.

Awi Usdi, Little Deer

(A CHEROKEE STORY)

The Tsa-la-gi Indians lived in parts of what is now Alabama, North and South Carolina, Georgia, Kentucky, Tennessee, Virginia, and West Virginia. "Tsa-la-gi" sounded like "Cherokee" to the French, and the name stuck.

Back when the world was young, the humans and the animal people could speak to each other. At first they lived in peace. The humans hunted the animals only when they needed food or skins to make clothing. Then the humans discovered the bow and arrow. With this new weapon, they could kill many animals quickly and with great ease. They began to kill animals when they did not need them for food or clothing. It seemed as if all the animals in the world would soon be exterminated.

The animals met in council. The bears decided they would have to fight back. "How can we do that?" said one of the bear warriors. "The humans will shoot us with their arrows before we come close to them." Old Bear, their chief, agreed. "That is true," he said. "We must learn how to use the same weapons they use." The bears made a very strong bow and fashioned arrows for it. But whenever they tried to use the bow, their long claws got in the way. "I will cut off my claws," said one of the bear warriors. He did so, and he was able to use the bow and arrow. His aim was good and he hit his mark every time.

"That is good," said Old Bear. "Now can you climb this tree?" The bear tried to climb the tree, but he failed. Old Bear shook his head. "This will not do. Without our claws, we cannot climb trees or hunt or dig for food. We must give up this idea of using the same weapons the humans use."

One by one, each of the animal groups met. One by one, they came to no conclusion. It seemed there was no way to fight back. But the last group to meet were the deer. Awi Usdi, Little Deer, was their leader. "I see what we must do," he said. "We cannot stop the humans from hunting animals. That is the way it was meant to be. However, the humans are not doing things in the right way. If they do not respect us and hunt when there is no need, they may kill us all. I shall go and tell the hunters what they must do. Whenever they wish to kill a deer, they must prepare a ceremony. They must ask me for permission to kill one of us. After they kill a deer, they must show respect to its spirit and ask for pardon. If they do not do this, I shall track them down and make their limbs crippled with my magic. Then they will no longer be able to walk or shoot a bow and arrow."

Awi Usdi, Little Deer, did as he said. At night, he whispered into the ears of the hunters, telling them what they must do. When they awoke, some of the hunters thought they had been dreaming and they were not sure that the dream was a true one. Others, though, realized that Awi Usdi, Little Deer, had spoken to them. They did as he had told them. They hunted for the deer and other animals only when they needed food and clothing. They remembered to prepare in a ceremonial way, to ask permission before killing an animal and to ask pardon when an animal was killed.

The others continued to kill animals for no reason. Awi Usdi, Little Deer, came to them and, using his magic, crippled them with rheumatism. Before long, all of the hunters began to treat the animals with respect and followed Awi Usdi, Little Deer's, teachings.

So it is that the animals have survived to this day. Because of Awi Usdi, Little Deer, the Indian people show respect. To this day, even though the animals and people no longer can speak to each other as in the old days, the people still show respect and give thanks to the animals they must hunt.

A horse and rider who can communicate successfully can do anything!

Chapter 3

Relationship Training

THERE IS ONLY ONE THING THAT STANDS BETWEEN HORSE and rider performing as one creature; only one hurdle that separates the perfect combination of two- and four-legged; only one stumbling block that awaits the horse and rider who wish to act as one. It is communication. A horse and rider who can communicate successfully can do anything—*anything!*

Just as the Native American rider's ability to communicate with horses was nothing short of spectacular, so was the horse's ability to interpret commands given on an instant's notice. Because they were *iyuptala* (ee-yoo-PTAH-lah), *one with* each other, horse-and-rider teams navigated treacherous terrain; rode amongst herds of thousands of stampeding buffalo; and descended steep mountain slopes, sometimes fleeing from an enemy.

Itancan Does Not Hesitate

❖×❖×❖×❖×❖×❖×❖×❖×❖×❖×❖×❖×❖×❖

Many people are amazed that Kola climbs stairs and rides in elevators. These are not tricks that I've taught him. He does all these things because I never gave any reason for him to believe that he couldn't. The first set of stairs that we ever encountered was treated no differently than a grassy hill. I held his lead, did not change my pace, did not look back to see if he could make it, and simply walked up. I knew that these stairs provided good footing before I approached them with Kola. Because the itancan did not hesitate, neither did the rest of the "herd." Walking into our first elevator was like walking into a box stall. He has also developed, on his own, a fondness for jumping onto stages, some as high as 4 feet! I think it's because he's the biggest ham I know. The point is that if there is hesitation in the mind or body language of the itancan, the herd will act accordingly.

Do not only
point out the way, but lead the way.

—*Sioux*

44

If at any time horse and rider were not thinking and responding as one being, injury or death to one or both of them was likely.

Relationship Training is more than a technique for communicating with a horse. It's a system of beliefs. In Relationship Training, we communicate with horses using the language horses know best—the language of the herd. And in Relationship Training, we focus on the relationship between person and horse rather than focusing on the results of training. Relationship Training is not rider teaching horse. Nor is it horse teaching rider. Rather, it is rider creating the right environment for horse and rider to understand each other.

In Relationship Training, we focus on the relationship between person and horse rather than focusing on the results of training.

Horses Know

❖X❖X❖X❖X❖X❖X❖X❖X❖X❖X❖X❖X❖X❖

Too often, riders view their animals as students and can't seem to understand why those animals don't "get it," when in fact, their horses already know it. Believe it or not, many horse owners have said, "My horse does not know how to go right," or "My horse won't stop." Think about these statements for a moment. Horses know how to do everything that is possible for them to do from the day that they are born. It is the rider who has the problem communicating. Horses do not need to be taught how to stop, turn, or spin around in a circle. Riders must be taught how to communicate these requests to their horses in an understandable way.

Sgt R Byrd

Teachers not only teach,
but they also learn.

—*Asa-ki-waki, Sauk*

Wisdom

No encyclopedia of horsemanship exists from the continent's first great horsemen. So many different tribes inhabited North America that it would not have been possible 200 years ago to collect and organize their *woksapa* (wo-KSAH-pah), or wisdom. But Native American wisdom about animals and our relationship to them is above and beyond that of many cultures. From this wisdom we can learn many things. Through storytelling, the wisdom of the elders has been passed down from generation to generation so that it could be added to the experiences of the people.

Native American wisdom about animals and our relationship to them is above and beyond that of many cultures.

I wanted to know more about relating to horses, so I asked Native American elders of different Nations for advice. I began to understand what it was that we do differently to get results with horses. If we understand what it means to be a horse, react like a horse, and relate to other things like a horse, then we can have a better relationship with a horse.

Almost every problem faced by the horse owner (except physical injuries or ailments) is due to an unbalanced relationship between horse and rider. In most cases, riders were not filling the position in the relationship that horses needed them to. A horse needs a leader. If he does not have a leader, he will become the leader. The best relationship between horse and rider grows when the rider is a strong leader. To be a strong leader, one must listen and understand.

Many tribes have a common custom that trains a person from a young age to listen. This custom takes on different forms in different tribes, but it can be explained by what's called the talking stick, a short stick of 12 to 18 inches, usually decorated with carvings. The person holding the stick is the only person permitted to talk. Once that person has finished, the stick is passed to the next person to talk. In the unlikely event that someone should interrupt the person holding the stick, the speaker would point at that person, and, in embarrassment, he would get up and leave the room.

It is said that the reason Creator gave two-leggeds two ears and one mouth was so that we could listen twice as much as we talk. Start listening.

Being "one with"

was a constant part

of Native American life.

Chapter 4

Being *Iyuptala*, One With, a Horse

TO KNOW WHAT IT MEANS TO BE *ONE WITH* ANOTHER BEING, imagine an eagle soaring in the wind. The eagle doesn't glide on top of, below, or alongside the wind, but is actually inside the wind. Every shift in the wind affects the eagle, and every beat of the eagle's wings moves the air currents around him. The soaring eagle becomes a small part of the wind. He moves with the ever-shifting winds. He is *iyuptala*, one with the wind.

Being *one with* was once a constant part of Native American life. The people were one with their environment, one with Mother Earth, and above all, one with Creator. So basic was this way of being in the world that words such as *trust, belief, faith,* and *promise* did not exist because their antonyms—words of opposite meaning (mistrust, disbelief, faithlessness, and lies)—also did not exist.

Every action of the Native American was based on his total trust in the environment. Never will you touch a fire that will not burn you. Never will you see rain that is not wet, and never will you see a wolf who is really a sheep. Natural things do not lie. A breech in trust was unthinkable. Trust was not the exception but the rule.

Natural things show trust in an entirely different way from humans. We must understand both types of trust before we embark on a relationship with a horse.

Most animals are born with the understanding to trust everything.

Most animals are born with the understanding to trust everything until there is a reason not to trust. Native Americans learned to trust in the animal way. Unfortunately, the experience of being *one with* has been lost by the majority of people living in the twentieth century. Far from feeling at one with our environment, one with Mother Earth, or even one with Creator, we learn from a very young age to trust nothing that has not first earned our trust.

In May 1966, a team of scientists went to the Galápagos Islands to study the animals there. The team was amazed by the animals! Most of the animals had never seen humans before. Birds landed on the scientists' shoulders; sea lions sunbathed next to them. Any species, even those with young, could be approached without difficulty. It was not until the scientists began trapping, collecting, and tagging the animals that the animals' behavior changed dramatically. After the animals were given a reason not to trust, they began treating humans as predators rather than neighbors.

Another example of this natural trust can be seen in the relationships turtles have with most animals. Most turtles and tortoises have managed somehow to keep the trust of much of the animal kingdom. Because they have never breached this trust, they are generally treated with indifference. If for some reason turtles and tortoises across the globe started biting the toes and legs and fins of passers-by, the animal kingdom's attitude toward turtles and tortoises would change. Here is a Sioux story about turtles.

How Turtle Flew South for the Winter

(A SIOUX STORY)

It was the time of year when the leaves start to fall from the aspens. Turtle was walking around when he saw many birds gathering together in the trees. They were making a lot of noise and Turtle was curious.

"Hey," Turtle said, "what's happening?"

"Don't you know?" the birds asked. "We're getting ready to fly to the south for winter."

"Why are you going to do that?" Turtle asked.

"Don't you know anything?" the birds said. "Soon it's going to be very cold here and the snow will fall. There won't be much food to eat. Down south it will be warm. Summer lives there all of the time and there's plenty of food."

As soon as they mentioned the food, Turtle became even more interested. "Can I come with you?" he asked.

"You have to fly to go south," said the birds. "You are a turtle and you can't fly." But Turtle would not give up. "Isn't there some way you could take me along?" He begged and pleaded. Finally the birds agreed just to get him to stop asking.

"Look here," the birds said, "can you hold onto a stick hard with your mouth?"

Originally the Sioux lived in the northern Plains. The Ojibwa-French word "Sioux" means "little snakes." It's no wonder the Sioux prefer the names Dakota, Nakota, or Lakota, which refer to their different dialects, regions, and economies.

"That's no problem at all," Turtle said. "Once I grab onto something no one can make me let go until I am ready."

"Good," said the birds. "Then you hold on hard to this stick. These two birds here will each grab one end of it in their claws. That way they can carry you along. But remember, you have to keep your mouth shut!"

"That's easy," said Turtle. "Now let's go south where Summer keeps all that food." Turtle grabbed onto the middle of the stick and two big birds came and grabbed each end. They flapped their wings hard and lifted Turtle off the ground.

Soon they were high in the sky and headed toward the south. Turtle had never been so high off the ground before, but he liked it. He could look down and see how small everything seemed. But before they had gone too far, he began to wonder where they were. He wondered what the lake was down below him and what those hills were. He wondered how far they had come and how far they would have to go to get to the south where Summer lived. He wanted to ask the two birds who were carrying him, but he couldn't talk with his mouth closed.

Turtle rolled his eyes. But the two birds just kept on flying. Then Turtle tried waving his legs at them, but they acted as if they didn't even notice. Now Turtle was getting upset. If they were going to take him south, then the least they could do was tell him where they were now!

"Mmmph," Turtle said, trying to get their attention. It didn't work. Finally, Turtle lost his temper.

"Why don't you listen to. . . ." but that was all he said, for as soon as he opened his mouth to speak, he started to fall.

Down and down he fell, a long long way. He was so frightened that he pulled his legs and his head into his shell to protect himself! When he hit the ground he hit it so hard that his shell cracked. He was lucky that he hadn't been killed, but he ached all over. He ached so much that he crawled into a nearby pond, swam down to the bottom and dug into to the mud to get as far away from the sky as he possibly could. Then he fell asleep and he slept all through the winter and didn't wake up until the spring.

So it is that today only the birds fly south to the land where summer lives while turtles, who all have cracked shells now, sleep through the winter.

If there were such a thing as a trust scale, the horse would fall somewhere between a dog and cow. Most horses are very trusting, yet it does not take much for them to lose that trust. This thought must be in the front of every rider's mind.

A horse's trust in people can be lost in any number of ways. If a person loses his temper and hits a horse, that person is on his way to creating a horse who will not trust his head to be touched again.

Remember, the rider is the itancan, the leader. He has chosen and earned that title on the condition that he will lead his two-member herd safely. If he begins to breach that trust by not acting responsibly and in the itancan manner, he will be replaced. Who will replace him? The other member of his herd, the horse.

Most horses are very trusting, but the rider must remember that he is itancan.

Teaching

While traveling around the country, speaking and performing at pow-wows and cultural festivals, I learned as much as I could about horsemanship from the local tribe's elders. I was raised alongside horses, and while on the road I found it hard to stay away from them. I discovered that no matter what part of the country I was in, someone could direct me to the local "Indian authority on horses." It is to these authorities that I owe much of my knowledge of the old ways concerning horses.

These old ways of horsemanship are fairly simple and focus on the basics. They rely on the rider's ability to lead. If a rider isn't confident enough to do something, he should not ask his horse to follow his lead.

When a horse accepts a rider as itancan, the rider must reinforce his leader status on a regular basis. Every time he works with his horse, he must do things exactly the same way, even very small things. He wants to send messages to his horse in the same way so the horse will always understand him. Being consistent is important. Without consistency, you will get nowhere.

Relationship Training usually requires working with a horse for no more than 30–40 minutes at a time. But these must be 30–40 minutes of undivided attention and commitment to building the relationship. A half hour of solid concentration and commitment can be just as strenuous as a 3- or 4-hour trail ride.

Time

A horse and rider acting as one is the most sought-after skill for most all riders. Being one with a horse requires open, two-way communication between horse and rider. It does not come quickly. To build a true relationship with open communication, specific tools are needed. The most important tool is time.

It takes time to build relationships. It takes time to strengthen friendships. A rider must want to spend time with his horse. If his desire to develop a relationship with a horse is nothing more than an empty wish, then the time to do so will never happen. And just because he happens to be in the same space as his horse doesn't mean he's using time as a tool. Hand grazing, taking his horse for a walk, grooming (for no purpose other than to connect with his horse), and hanging out in the pasture are all opportunities to deepen the relationship with his horse. Barn chores, feeding, and mindless longeing are not.

Living in Close Quarters

×·×·×·×·×·×·×·×·×·×·×·×·×·×·×·×·×

When I had the opportunity to spend two years traveling, giving clinics and seminars, I came to appreciate the impact that time had on my relationship with Kola. I lived in the front half of a 16-foot stock trailer, and Kola lived in the back. Our quarters were separated by a steel bar that came up to Kola's chest. I soon learned that, like humans, Kola snored and grunted in his sleep, and had nightmares. Living with a horse, you learn to recognize contentment, boredom, frustration—the same things you'd learn about a human were you to spend a lot of time together. I became accustomed to Kola's habits in about a month, and soon found no reason to trade in our two-bedroom condo-on-wheels. I'm glad I didn't, because living so closely with my horse helped me learn a valuable lesson: When developing a relationship with your horse, there is no substitute for spending time together.

All plants are
our brothers and sisters.
They talk to us and
if we listen, we can hear them.

—Arapaho

Let's travel back to the early 1700s and take a look at how much time the continent's greatest horsemen spent with their horses. Imagine you're a Native American living with your family in a camp with 80 or so other families. Your horses (not tied) are perfectly happy to share with you the meadows found just outside camp. As you gather herbs and berries, the four-legged members of your tribe graze at your side. While you bathe, the itancan leads the herd to the river. When the horses have quenched their thirst, the itancan takes a drink as well. Occasionally, a foal bounds through camp with children close behind trying to grab her short, wiry tail.

Your nights are spent sleeping in your family lodge, a cone-shaped tepee. Through the smoke opening at the top of the tepee, you can see the stars. The constant murmur of the herd provides a background for your every thought and dream. A *sakehanska* (sha–KAY–han–SKAH), a long-claws, or grizzly bear, approaches the camp. With grunts and whinnies the herd alerts everyone to the danger. The young men silently leave the tepees to frighten the predator away. When the men return, you can hear the mares calming and reassuring their young.

What kind of relationship would you have with your horse if you both lived in the 1760s? Seeing your horse's emotions and responses to daily events would help you have a greater understanding of your horse and a deeper appreciation for your horse.

Simple yet rewarding, spending a day with a horse is an important exercise. It requires no special talents or skills, but the rider gets dramatic results.

To spend a day with his horse, the rider starts just before dawn. The rider enters the barn or pasture and finds a comfortable place to watch his horse quietly. Horses in a barn or pasture will likely notice a human and may expect to be fed. The rider remains still. He does not talk to or pat his horse or the others. He is there to observe. He becomes an invisible part of his horse's surroundings as best he can. He takes notes. He pays attention to what his horse is doing and why. He asks himself questions and answers his questions by watching his horse. He builds a stronger understanding of his horse.

Although the rider is quiet while watching his horse, the horse will probably notice him.

Spending time watching a horse helps build understanding between horse and rider.

Some questions he asks are: Who in the herd is my horse closest to? Does my horse touch the other horses? Does he respond to other horses touching him? Is he a picky eater, choosing only the best grass from each section of the pasture, or does he "sweep" the entire area? Where is his favorite place to nap? Does my horse stay with the herd or does he go off on his own or with a special friend? Does he "talk" to his herd mates? Does he watch as the others gallop? Does he start herd gallops? How does he react to dogs and cats? Does he play in the water trough, chew on tree branches or fence boards, paw the dirt, shake his head a lot, or scratch himself on fence posts? Where on my horse's body does he sweat the most? Does he have a favorite place to go to the bathroom? How many times a day does my horse roll?

These are just some of the questions a rider could answer by spending a single day watching his horse. If he did this exercise regularly, he'd see that some of the answers even change with the horse's moods, physical condition, and the seasons.

For a strong relationship, a rider should get to know his horse as well as he possibly can. By learning what motivates his horse's actions, a rider can begin to understand the best way to communicate his requests to his horse. Horses are individuals, and unless we understand the individual we cannot expect the individual to understand us.

Tools

Tools can be used to create, repair, adjust, or improve any part of the relationship that we are developing. A tool is anything used during training or riding that a horse does not usually encounter when he is on his own. Tools include the rider, along with his voice, weight, movements, and hands. It is important that a horse be 100 percent comfortable with the tools used to communicate with him.

The first tool to introduce to a horse is the rider's hands. The rider needs to be able to touch every part of his horse's body with his hands. To get his horse used to his hands, the rider uses his hands like a brush

The first tool to introduce to a horse is the rider's hands.

all over his horse's body. He pays close attention to his horse's reactions. The rider may touch areas that make his horse uncomfortable. These sensitive areas may be caused by health problems, scars, or bad or good experiences. For example, a horse who has enjoyed close physical contact with his pasture mates may display affection and enjoyment when hands pass over his withers and mane.

Once the rider identifies sensitive areas, he focuses his attention on them. If he discovers that his horse is not comfortable with his ears being touched, he uses slow, deliberate, firm movements to gain his horse's trust in this matter. The rider rubs his horse's ears firmly. He does not grab or squeeze them. He watches his horse's reaction. If the horse throws his head up or takes a step back, he may be telling the rider "that's enough." The rider should immediately stop touching his horse's ears and instead move his hands down the horse's neck and continue stroking. The rider then goes back up to his horse's ears several times and stops immediately when the horse gives the signal that he has had enough. The rider keeps his touches soft and firm so he doesn't tickle the horse. The ear-touching exercise is repeated for many days until the horse doesn't mind being touched all over his body.

Once the horse is totally comfortable with the rider's hands all over his body, the rider can do the same with all the tools he will be using. He'll move on to the headstall, bit, blanket, and every other tool he asks his horse to accept. He allows his horse to smell, lick, or even chew on any of the tools. Horses are tactile animals and investigate things and situations with their muzzles and mouths.

When the horse becomes almost bored with all the tools and accepts them as commonplace, the rider is ready to move on to another step in Relationship Training. But if the horse becomes fearful of a tool again, the rider will go through this exercise again until the horse is comfortable and trusts the rider and the tool.

Spoken messages are saved for urgent communication.

Talking to Animals

You can communicate with animals in three ways: by talking to them, by touching them, and by focusing. When you're focusing, you're concentrating hard on a goal. Animals can sense your concentration and will respond to what you're focusing on. When you are first learning to communicate with an animal, a combination of talking, touching, and focusing is usually necessary.

Imagine a scale of one to ten that measures the importance of a message you give an animal. Ten is the most urgent. A focused message is about a three on the scale. A touching message is a six. A talking message is a nine or ten. Without this scale of urgency, you will communicate all messages equally, and your animal will become bored or confused. For instance, if you use the same message—at the same intensity—to slow a horse to a walk as you do to avoid running into a briar patch, you will end up with many thorns in your britches. However, if you yell "Whoa!" every time you would like to slow down a little bit, your horse will start ignoring you.

Spoken Messages

Horses are not vocal creatures the way humans are. We think and communicate in words, whereas horses use body language and focus. Horses usually vocalize only to establish territory, convey danger, or comfort peers. Riders who use a lot of talking commands in their riding are communicating with their horses as if they were humans. Spoken messages should be saved for urgent communication. The best times to use spoken commands are to stop or start a horse abruptly.

The types of words used to convey either stop or go are important. Riders can use any words they like, but the more successful communicators make sure that the words they choose are ones they use already. In a situation where a rider has to make a quick stop, he doesn't want to have to rack his brain to remember his stop word. In fact, these cues do not have to be real words but can be mere sounds, such as the commands used by mule or draft horse drivers. The words will flow more naturally if they're already a natural part of your speech.

The rider also has to make sure his horse can tell the difference between the stop and the go words. Horses are widely thought to perceive syllable and vowel sounds more clearly than anything else. With this in mind, we should not use *whoa* and *go*. I use a word pronounced whee-cha for my *go* command. This is a Comanche word that usually conveys celebration or excitement. For *stop*, I use a word pronounced shkee, a Cherokee slang word that roughly translates to *thank you*.

Touching Messages

Horses are aware of their surroundings at all times. They need to always be on the lookout for animals who hunt them. Horses also are aware of everything their riders are doing. It takes only a slight shift of weight in the right direction to tell a horse to do any number of things. This shift in weight and other physical communications are called touching messages. Some of the messages that physical communication

A rider's slight shift of weight is a touching message.

conveys are stand, stop, start, slow down, speed up, step, jump, turn, and back up.

Horses understand touching messages well. Using touch to communicate to a horse is best in most situations. The worst use of touching messages is kicking a horse to get him to move or to move faster. The best use of touching messages is to reinforce your focused messages.

Focused Messages

Focus is an ability that both humans and horses possess. A lot of concentration is needed to communicate messages to a horse using focus. You've experienced focus before. One example of focus is when you sense that someone is watching you. That person is using focus to get your attention.

Whenever we try to understand something, we focus on it. If we don't understand a shape or object we focus our eyes. If we can't hear something, we focus our ears. And if we don't understand an idea, we focus our minds.

Horses know what we are focusing on. To prove this, I tried the following test. I got on a horse and sat as comfortably as I could. I looked at the back of the horse's head and thought *Do something!*

but I didn't move my body. I thought this command very hard as if there were something specific I wanted my horse to do, but I did not concentrate on any one task. Almost immediately an ear swiveled back toward me and my horse took a step. By pointing an ear in my direction, my horse was saying *I sense that you want me to do something, but without physical reinforcement, I don't know what it is.* By taking a step, my horse was trying something out, asking *Did you want me to go this way?*

Native American horsemen had no option but to focus on what they wanted their horses to do next. When riding amid a herd of buffalo that was sometimes thousands strong, there was no time to think about commands, body movements, or spoken messages. Those buffalo hunters relied both on their horses' ability to sense what their riders wanted to do, and their horses' knowledge of the safest and most efficient way to do it.

Without focus, a rider may be sending mixed messages to his horse. If what he wants his horse to do is not important enough to focus on, his horse may feel that it is not important enough to do. Once a horse can decipher a rider's focused messages, the rider can lead him through some basic maneuvers—halt, walk, turn—then move on to more refined maneuvers, such as asking for only a few steps at a time. If the rider is paying attention to his horse's communications, he will know when he is ready to move on to more challenging tasks.

Uncle! Uncle! Leksi! Leksi!

(A LAKOTA STORY)

[leh-K'SHEE leh-K'SHEE]

One morning in winter, the sun failed to appear on the eastern horizon. A council meeting was held. The elders decided that a scouting party of four should ride to the east to find out what had happened and to evaluate the situation. One of the scouts, Walking Crow, thought that since the sun had last been seen on the western horizon, it must still be hiding there, so he rode west. The other three scouts returned 10 days later, having found no answers. Walking Crow did not return after 10 days. He did not return after 20 days, and he did not return after 30 days. Still, the sky was dark.

Laughing Beaver, Walking Crow's nephew, became concerned about his Uncle. Laughing Beaver's father had been killed in a skirmish, and Walking Crow had taken him in as his own son. After 30 days of darkness, Laughing Beaver decided he would look for his uncle. He gathered his things, mounted his pony, and rode to the west.

The rest of the village held daily prayer councils and sweats in hopes of bringing back the sun. After a while, Walking Crow and Laughing Beaver were counted among the dead. They were not spoken of in the village. Then, after three years of darkness, the sun returned in the east as it had always done. The people were happy and the elders held a special ceremony thanking Creator. The ceremony was held at the eastern-most part of the people's range in honor of the sun's return to the east. During the prayers, a young boy pointed out two strange creatures grazing in the valley below. They appeared to be ponies with scouts on their backs, but the scouts had no legs. They seemed to be attached to the ponies' backs. The medicine man, Big Tree, said that those two strange creatures were Walking Crow and Laughing Beaver and their ponies, and that because the two scouts had spent three years on their ponies' backs in the darkness, they and their ponies had become one. Big Tree also said that Walking Crow and Laughing Beaver must have chased the sun all the way from the west to the east, and that their names should remain in the people's hearts always.

The Lakota legend *Leksi! Leksi!* was told to young riders before they practiced their focal abilities with horses. Young riders were told to take their horses out at night and maneuver them using only focus. If at any time they felt frightened or confused, they could call out, *Leksi! Leksi!*, and Walking Crow and Laughing Beaver would guide them home safely.

This is a good activity for any rider who wants to strengthen a bond with a horse. A moonlit night can make this experience extra special. But the rider should feel comfortable riding in the dark. Being afraid or confused while riding a horse damages rather than strengthens the trust and bond the rider has with him.

Practicing focal abilities at night works best in open fields or pastures. A rider must choose the riding area carefully and check it during the daytime for gopher holes, rocks, wire or boards on the ground, debris, broken fences, and other hazards.

At first it's best for the rider to choose a night with a full or near-full moon, low wind, and no cloud cover to obstruct the moon. He should mount his horse in the field and allow a few moments for both him and the horse to get used to training at night. Horses are more comfortable in the dark than most humans, so it's the rider who must concentrate on relaxing. You may think that a horse will not respond as quickly at night as he does during the day. But riding cues are quickly understood by horses whether it's day or night. The darkness does make it more important for there to be a strong focal connection between horse and rider.

Riding bareback

is the ultimate

test of balance.

The way to test this focal connection is for horse and rider to zigzag across and up and down the field. The rider should focus on a spot somewhere in the field and see if his horse will come within 10 to 20 yards of this spot. The rider should praise the horse every time the horse is successful.

Most important to every rider is safety. If you ride or are planning to ride horses, please wear a helmet or hard hat and any other appropriate safety gear.

Balance

A rider needs balance to be one with his horse. Riding bareback is the ultimate test of balance. To establish a safe, comfortable, confident, balanced, and effective position while riding bareback—the rider begins riding at a walk with his shoulders square over his hips, his back relaxed and straight, and his chest open. His hips should absorb and follow the motion of the horse, and his shoulders should be relaxed and relatively still so that his upper body is not rocking around as the horse walks.

Once on a horse's back, a rider relaxes and watches for signs that his horse is focusing on him. For example, one or both of the horse's ears swivel back toward the rider; the horse stands quietly, waiting for communication from the rider; and the horse is not calling to or paying attention to his herd mates or wandering around. The rider then focuses on a specific spot where he would like to go. He may lean forward slightly when trying to direct his horse to move forward. That's okay. When focusing, a rider's natural tendency is to shift his body toward the direction in which he wants to go. If the horse should take half a step in the direction that the rider is focusing on without responding to any previous learned physical cues, the horse is rewarded immediately and generously with treats and a pat.

Praise

Native American elders teach that when someone does a good thing, he or she should be rewarded. Our horses are no exception. Treats, pats, hugs, and kind words are regular parts of Relationship Training.

It's possible for a horse to become spoiled, so riders must avoid using hugs and treats as bribes. But they should tuck a few treats into their pockets, and when they find themselves saying to their horse *You did a great job—I wish there were some way I could show my appreciation,* they reach into their pockets. It is best to give treats to a horse by placing them on the ground or in the horse's feed bin. This prevents the horse from learning any bad habits such as nibbling at fingers or expecting a treat every time someone reaches out a hand.

You can see that a special bond exists between people and animals.

Chapter 5

Teaching with Patience

YOU CAN SEE THAT A SPECIAL BOND EXISTS BETWEEN PEOPLE and animals. Animals give people love and companionship. They provide us with clothing, food, drink, transportation, power, tools, jewelry, medicines, and shelter. Can you imagine a world without dogs, cats, horses, cows, sheep, pigs, deer, dolphins, or whales?

Just because animals don't use words to communicate like we do doesn't mean that animals are not smart. Everyone knows about the learning abilities of dogs. They're master communicators! We talk to our dogs and they understand us. Eventually, we learn to understand their whines and barks. There are Seeing-Eye dogs for the blind, dogs for the hearing-impaired, and dogs who have saved their owners from burning buildings.

Horses have incredible memories. If intelligence were purely graded on the ability to remember and use information, I believe horses would be considered far more intelligent than humans.

Have you been to a marine aquarium lately? Aquariums are filled with animals such as whales, seals, and dolphins who have highly developed learning abilities, motor skills, and social awareness. Or how about the zoo? The intricate social behavior, communication, and learning skills of monkeys, baboons, chimpanzees, and other apes in the wild and at any zoo reveal very smart animals.

The way many people train their animals is by asking or by telling them what to do and expecting them to obey. They tell their pets to sit, stay, giddyap, whoa, roll over, come, and heel. When the animals do what they are told, they're rewarded. When they disobey, they're punished. They are merely performing a task because someone is telling them to do it. How do you feel when you are around someone who is always telling you what to do?

The problem with telling as communication is that the only two options given for performance are reward and punishment. The reward is not necessarily something you want, but rather something the teller wishes to give you. Punishment is nothing more than the result of *Do this or you will suffer in some way.*

When communicating with horses, always be aware of their great memory. Telling a horse to do something does not make for a very good relationship with your horse. Asking has its place in communication, but asking can be a trap. Asking is a nice way to try to get your horse to do something if you're trying to help the horse learn. But unfortunately, most riders ask in the wrong way and for the wrong reasons—just to get results.

Teaching with patience, *waonspekiye* [wah-OON-spay-KEE-yay], means treating your horse the same way that you would treat a younger child who has difficulty learning or grasping new concepts. If you allow your horse understanding, concern, and patience, you will get amazing results. Many of the same methods I use in Relationship Training with horses are used in special education classes to teach learning-disabled students. These are methods such as giving immediate rewards, taking many small steps rather than a few large ones to teach a new idea, and basing each lesson on the success of the previous lesson.

Native Americans and Horses Today

Many Native Americans have chosen to continue their special relationship with the horse, even in today's super technological environment. The paths they have taken are wide and various. Some people keep a small string of horses on their property and continue training horses and horse owners. Others have huge ranches with hundreds of horses and herds of buffalo. Their lives are similar to those of cattle ranchers. It's tough, hard work.

Other Native Americans have chosen a more pleasurable route. They introduce relaxed, happy vacationers to Native American sights on scenic horseback rides through such historic and beautiful places as Canyon de Chelly National Monument in Arizona. And others work within the Native American community, using horses to help kids who are having problems with drugs and alcohol. The kids are taught how to care for a horse. If the kids can show over the course of a year that they can stay clean and are capable of the big responsibility of caring for a horse, they're allowed to keep the horse. That's quite a prize! But no matter what path the Native American has chosen for himself, the bond between him and the horse has remained firm and strong and will endure no matter what.

Many Native Americans

have chosen to continue

their special relationship

with the horse.

Understanding, teaching, and leadership are the keys to a strong relationship with horses.

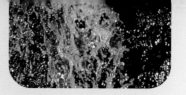

Glossary

Brother—the word *brother* has special meaning for Native Americans. It means more than a relationship between two relatives. The legends of several tribes have brothers involved with astronomy, geology, weather, and the seasons. To be called a brother takes on great meaning in tribal culture.

Coup—a French word meaning touch

Hunkapi **[hoon-KAH-pee]**—being related to everyone

Itancan **[ee-TAHN-chun]**—leader

Iyuptala **[ee-yoo-PTAH-lah]**—being one with

Kola—a friend with whom you could face many enemies. The word *kola* is not normally used for animals but is reserved for human brother-warriors. In using *kola* as a descriptor of their relationship to their horses, Native American warriors acknowledged their horses' equal status as brother-warrior.

Leksi **[leh-K'SHEE]**—uncle

Longeing—using a longe line, a whip, and the trainer's voice, longeing is a way of training a horse to respond to the trainer's voice while he is standing on the ground

Nez Percé—pierced nose; Native American tribe who bred horses

Palousa—the word from which the name Appaloosa is derived

Sakehanska [**sha-KAY-hahn-SKAH**]—grizzly bear; also known as long-claws by some Native tribes

Travois—two large sticks crossed and tied to a dog or horse's back, forming a travois on which family belongings could be carried

Waonspekiye [**wah-OON-spay-KEE-yay**]—teaching with patience

Waunca [**wah-OON-kah**]—imitator or follower

Woksapa [**wo-KSAH-pah**]—wisdom

Selected Bibliography >>>>>>

Anderson, Madelyn Klein. *The Nez Percé.* New York: Franklin Watts, 1994.

Boulet, Susan Seddon. *Shaman: The Paintings of Susan Seddon Boulet.* San Francisco: Pomegranate Artbooks, 1989.

Caduto, Michael J., and Joseph Bruchac. *Keepers of the Animals: Native American Stories and Wildlife Activities.* Golden, CO: Fulcrum Publishing, 1991.

Featherly, Jay. *Mustangs: Wild Horses of the American West.* Minneapolis: Carolrhoda Books, 1986.

Freedman, Russell. *Children of the Wild West.* New York: Houghton Mifflin, 1983.

Goble Paul. *The Gift of the Sacred Dog.* New York: Simon & Schuster, 1980.

Goble, Paul. *The Girl Who Loved Wild Horses.* New York: Simon & Schuster, 1978.

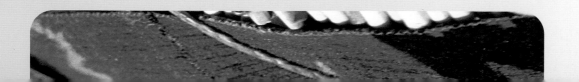

Grutman, Jewel, and Gay Matthaei. *The Ledgerbook of Thomas Blue Eagle.* Charlottesville, VA: Thomasson-Grant, Inc., 1994.

Haines, Frances. *The Nez Percés.* Norman, OK: University of Oklahoma Press, 1955.

Hoxie, Frederick, E., ed. *Encyclopedia of North American Indians.* New York: Houghton Mifflin Co., 1996.

Mishkin, Bernard. *Rank and Warfare Among the Plains Indians.* Lincoln, Nebraska: University of Nebraska Press, 1940.

Moorhead, Carol Ann. *Wild Horses.* Niwot, CO: Denver Museum of Natural History, 1994.

Richardson, Bill and Dona. *The Appaloosa.* Hollywood, CA: Wilshire Book Co., 1969.

Ruby, Robert H. and John A. Brown. *A Guide to the Indian Tribes of the Pacific Northwest.* Norman, Oklahoma: University of Oklahoma Press, 1992.

Sams, Jamie and David Carson. *Medicine Cards: The Discovery of Power Through the Ways of Animals.* Santa Fe, NM: Bear & Company, 1988.

Stroud, Virginia. *Doesn't Fall off His Horse.* New York: Penguin Books USA, 1994.

Time-Life Editors. *The Way of the Warrior.* Alexandria, VA: Time-Life Books, 1993.

Yolen, Jane and Barry Moser. *Sky Dogs.* San Diego: Harcourt Brace Jovanovich, 1990.